This Journal Belongs to

You're Gorgeous & Awesome

A MOTHER'S LOVE IS UNCONDITIONAL AND ONLY GROWS STRONGER OVER A **LIFETIME**

> "A mother is your first Friend, your best Friend, your forever Friend."

"Mother is a verb. It's something you do, not just who you are."

By Dorothy Canfield Fisher

"*A mother is your first Friend, your best Friend, your forever Friend.*"

"Mother is a verb. It's something you do, not just who you are."

By Dorothy Canfield Fisher

"Moms are the people who know us the best and love us the most."

"A mother's love is the fuel that enables a normal Human being to do the impossible." By Marion C. Garretty

> "Mother's love is peace. It need not be acquired; it need not be deserved." — By Erich Fromm

"For a mother is the only person on earth who can divide her love among 10 children and each child still have all her love."

"A mother is she who can take the place of all others but whose place no one else can take."

— By cardinal Mermillod

Date:

Quote Of The Day

Today I am truly grateful for...

Here's what would make today great...

I am...

Some amazing things that happened today...

Some amazing things that happened today...

What could I have done to make today even better?

"A mother is she who can take the place of all others but whose place no one else can take."

By cardinal Mermillod

Date: _____

Quote Of The Day
_____
_____

Today I am truly grateful for...
_____
_____
_____
_____
_____

Here's what would make today great...
_____
_____
_____
_____
_____

I am...
_____
_____
_____

Some amazing things that happened today...
_____
_____

Some amazing things that happened today...
_____
_____

What could I have done to make today even better?
_____
_____

Recipe:

Rating: ☆☆☆☆☆ Difficulty: ☆☆☆☆☆ Prep Time: Cook Time:

Ingredients:

Cooking Instructions:

Thoughts and Notes:

Prayer journal

DATE

TODAY'S PASSAGE

PREACHER

SERMON TOPIC

NOTES

KEY VERSES

PRAYER

KEY POINTS

APPLICATION

Notes

Date: _____

Quote Of The Day

_____
_____
_____

Today I am truly grateful for...

_____
_____
_____
_____
_____

Here's what would make today great...

_____
_____
_____
_____
_____

I am...

_____
_____

Some amazing things that happened today...

_____
_____

Some amazing things that happened today...

_____
_____

What could I have done to make today even better?

_____
_____

Recipe:

Rating: ☆☆☆☆☆ Difficulty: ☆☆☆☆☆ Prep Time: Cook Time:

Ingredients:

Cooking Instructions:

Thoughts and Notes:

Date:

Quote Of The Day
_____
_____
_____

Today I am truly grateful for...
_____
_____
_____
_____
_____

Here's what would make today great...
_____
_____
_____
_____
_____

I am...
_____
_____
_____

Some amazing things that happened today...
_____
_____

Some amazing things that happened today...
_____
_____

What could I have done to make today even better?
_____
_____

Recipe:

Rating: ☆☆☆☆☆ Difficulty: ☆☆☆☆☆ Prep Time: Cook Time:

Ingredients:

Cooking Instructions:

Thoughts and Notes:

Date:

Quote Of The Day
_____
_____
_____

Today I am truly grateful for...
_____
_____
_____
_____
_____
_____

Here's what would make today great...
_____
_____
_____
_____
_____
_____

I am...
_____
_____
_____

Some amazing things that happened today...
_____
_____

Some amazing things that happened today...
_____
_____

What could I have done to make today even better?
_____
_____

Recipe:

Rating: ☆☆☆☆☆ **Difficulty:** ☆☆☆☆☆ **Prep Time:**   **Cook Time:**

Ingredients:

Cooking Instructions:

Thoughts and Notes:

Prayer journal

DATE

TODAY'S PASSAGE   PREACHER   SERMON TOPIC

NOTES

KEY VERSES

PRAYER

KEY POINTS

APPLICATION

Notes

Date: _____

Quote Of The Day

Today I am truly grateful for...

Here's what would make today great...

I am...

Some amazing things that happened today...

Some amazing things that happened today...

What could I have done to make today even better?

Recipe:

Rating: ☆☆☆☆☆ Difficulty: ☆☆☆☆☆ Prep Time: Cook Time:

Ingredients:

Cooking Instructions:

Thoughts and Notes:

Date: _____

Quote Of The Day
_____
_____
_____

Today I am truly grateful for...
_____
_____
_____
_____
_____

Here's what would make today great...
_____
_____
_____
_____
_____

I am...
_____
_____
_____

Some amazing things that happened today...
_____
_____

Some amazing things that happened today...
_____
_____

What could I have done to make today even better?
_____
_____

Recipe:

Rating: ☆☆☆☆☆ Difficulty: ☆☆☆☆☆ Prep Time: Cook Time:

Ingredients:

Cooking Instructions:

Thoughts and Notes:

Prayer journal

DATE

TODAY'S PASSAGE

PREACHER

SERMON TOPIC

NOTES

PRAYER

KEY VERSES

KEY POINTS

APPLICATION

Notes

Date:

Quote Of The Day

Today I am truly grateful for...

Here's what would make today great...

I am...

Some amazing things that happened today...

Some amazing things that happened today...

What could I have done to make today even better?

Recipe:

Rating: ☆☆☆☆☆ Difficulty: ☆☆☆☆☆ Prep Time: Cook Time:

Ingredients:

Cooking Instructions:

Thoughts and Notes:

Prayer journal

DATE

TODAY'S PASSAGE   PREACHER   SERMON TOPIC

NOTES

KEY VERSES

PRAYER

KEY POINTS

APPLICATION

Notes

Guest List Planner

Name

Address

Telephone Number

E-mail Address

Gift

Save The Day Card Sent	Invitation Sent	R.S.V.P Received	Thank You Sent	Number Attending

Name

Address

Telephone Number

E-mail Address

Gift

Save The Day Card Sent	Invitation Sent	R.S.V.P Received	Thank You Sent	Number Attending

Name

Address

Telephone Number

E-mail Address

Gift

Save The Day Card Sent	Invitation Sent	R.S.V.P Received	Thank You Sent	Number Attending

Name

Address

Telephone Number

E-mail Address

Gift

Save The Day Card Sent	Invitation Sent	R.S.V.P Received	Thank You Sent	Number Attending

Name

Address

Telephone Number

E-mail Address

Gift

Save The Day Card Sent	Invitation Sent	R.S.V.P Received	Thank You Sent	Number Attending

Date:

Quote Of The Day

Today I am truly grateful for...

Here's what would make today great...

I am...

Some amazing things that happened today...

Some amazing things that happened today...

What could I have done to make today even better?

Recipe:

Rating: ☆☆☆☆☆ Difficulty: ☆☆☆☆☆ Prep Time: Cook Time:

Ingredients:

Cooking Instructions:

Thoughts and Notes:

Prayer journal

DATE

TODAY'S PASSAGE   PREACHER   SERMON TOPIC

NOTES

KEY VERSES

KEY POINTS

PRAYER

APPLICATION

Notes

Date: _____

Quote Of The Day

_____
_____

Today I am truly grateful for...

_____
_____
_____
_____

Here's what would make today great...

_____
_____
_____
_____

I am...

_____
_____

Some amazing things that happened today...

_____

Some amazing things that happened today...

_____
_____

What could I have done to make today even better?

_____
_____

Recipe:

Rating: ☆☆☆☆☆ **Difficulty:** ☆☆☆☆☆ **Prep Time:** **Cook Time:**

Ingredients:

Cooking Instructions:

Thoughts and Notes:

Prayer journal

DATE

TODAY'S PASSAGE   PREACHER   SERMON TOPIC

NOTES

PRAYER

KEY VERSES

KEY POINTS

APPLICATION

Notes

Guest List Planner

Name

Address

Telephone Number

E-mail Address

Gift

| Save The Day Card Sent | Invitation Sent | R.S.V.P Received | Thank You Sent | Number Attending |

Name

Address

Telephone Number

E-mail Address

Gift

| Save The Day Card Sent | Invitation Sent | R.S.V.P Received | Thank You Sent | Number Attending |

Name

Address

Telephone Number

E-mail Address

Gift

| Save The Day Card Sent | Invitation Sent | R.S.V.P Received | Thank You Sent | Number Attending |

Name

Address

Telephone Number

E-mail Address

Gift

| Save The Day Card Sent | Invitation Sent | R.S.V.P Received | Thank You Sent | Number Attending |

Name

Address

Telephone Number

E-mail Address

Gift

| Save The Day Card Sent | Invitation Sent | R.S.V.P Received | Thank You Sent | Number Attending |

Date:

Quote Of The Day

Today I am truly grateful for...

Here's what would make today great...

I am...

Some amazing things that happened today...

Some amazing things that happened today...

What could I have done to make today even better?

Recipe:

Rating: ☆☆☆☆☆ Difficulty: ☆☆☆☆☆ Prep Time: Cook Time:

Ingredients:

Cooking Instructions:

Thoughts and Notes:

Prayer journal

DATE _____

TODAY'S PASSAGE | PREACHER | SERMON TOPIC

NOTES
_____
_____
_____
_____
_____
_____
_____
_____
_____
_____
_____

KEY VERSES

PRAYER
_____
_____
_____
_____
_____
_____
_____
_____
_____
_____
_____
_____
_____
_____
_____
_____

KEY POINTS

APPLICATION

Notes

Date: _____

Quote Of The Day

_____
_____

Today I am truly grateful for...

_____
_____
_____
_____
_____

Here's what would make today great...

_____
_____
_____
_____
_____

I am...

_____
_____
_____

Some amazing things that happened today...

_____
_____

Some amazing things that happened today...

_____
_____

What could I have done to make today even better?

_____
_____

Recipe:

Rating: ☆☆☆☆☆ Difficulty: ☆☆☆☆☆ Prep Time: Cook Time:

Ingredients:

Cooking Instructions:

Thoughts and Notes:

Prayer journal

DATE

TODAY'S PASSAGE   PREACHER   SERMON TOPIC

NOTES

PRAYER

KEY VERSES

KEY POINTS

APPLICATION

Notes

Guest List Planner

Name

Address

Telephone Number

E-mail Address

Gift

Save The Day Card Sent	Invitation Sent	R.S.V.P Received	Thank You Sent	Number Attending

Name

Address

Telephone Number

E-mail Address

Gift

Save The Day Card Sent	Invitation Sent	R.S.V.P Received	Thank You Sent	Number Attending

Name

Address

Telephone Number

E-mail Address

Gift

Save The Day Card Sent	Invitation Sent	R.S.V.P Received	Thank You Sent	Number Attending

Name

Address

Telephone Number

E-mail Address

Gift

Save The Day Card Sent	Invitation Sent	R.S.V.P Received	Thank You Sent	Number Attending

Name

Address

Telephone Number

E-mail Address

Gift

Save The Day Card Sent	Invitation Sent	R.S.V.P Received	Thank You Sent	Number Attending

Date:

Quote Of The Day

Today I am truly grateful for...

Here's what would make today great...

I am...

Some amazing things that happened today...

Some amazing things that happened today...

What could I have done to make today even better?

Recipe:

Rating: ☆☆☆☆☆ **Difficulty:** ☆☆☆☆☆ **Prep Time:**   **Cook Time:**

Ingredients:

Cooking Instructions:

Thoughts and Notes:

Prayer journal

DATE

TODAY'S PASSAGE   PREACHER   SERMON TOPIC

NOTES

KEY VERSES

PRAYER

KEY POINTS

APPLICATION

Notes

Date:

Quote Of The Day

Today I am truly grateful for...

Here's what would make today great...

I am...

Some amazing things that happened today...

Some amazing things that happened today...

What could I have done to make today even better?

Recipe:

Rating: ☆☆☆☆☆ Difficulty: ☆☆☆☆☆ Prep Time: Cook Time:

Ingredients:

Cooking Instructions:

Thoughts and Notes:

Prayer journal

DATE

TODAY'S PASSAGE PREACHER SERMON TOPIC

NOTES

KEY VERSES

KEY POINTS

PRAYER

APPLICATION

Notes

Guest List Planner

Name

Address

Telephone Number

E-mail Address

Gift

| Save The Day Card Sent | Invitation Sent | R.S.V.P Received | Thank You Sent | Number Attending |

Name

Address

Telephone Number

E-mail Address

Gift

| Save The Day Card Sent | Invitation Sent | R.S.V.P Received | Thank You Sent | Number Attending |

Name

Address

Telephone Number

E-mail Address

Gift

| Save The Day Card Sent | Invitation Sent | R.S.V.P Received | Thank You Sent | Number Attending |

Name

Address

Telephone Number

E-mail Address

Gift

| Save The Day Card Sent | Invitation Sent | R.S.V.P Received | Thank You Sent | Number Attending |

Name

Address

Telephone Number

E-mail Address

Gift

| Save The Day Card Sent | Invitation Sent | R.S.V.P Received | Thank You Sent | Number Attending |

Date: _____

Quote Of The Day
_____
_____
_____

Today I am truly grateful for...
_____
_____
_____
_____
_____

Here's what would make today great...
_____
_____
_____
_____
_____

I am...
_____
_____

Some amazing things that happened today...
_____
_____

Some amazing things that happened today...
_____
_____

What could I have done to make today even better?
_____
_____

Recipe:

Rating: ☆☆☆☆☆ **Difficulty:** ☆☆☆☆☆ **Prep Time:** **Cook Time:**

Ingredients:

Cooking Instructions:

Thoughts and Notes:

Prayer journal

DATE

TODAY'S PASSAGE   PREACHER   SERMON TOPIC

NOTES

KEY VERSES

PRAYER

KEY POINTS

APPLICATION

Notes

Date: _____

Quote Of The Day

_____
_____
_____

Today I am truly grateful for...

_____
_____
_____
_____
_____

Here's what would make today great...

_____
_____
_____
_____
_____

I am...

_____
_____
_____

Some amazing things that happened today...

_____
_____

Some amazing things that happened today...

_____
_____

What could I have done to make today even better?

_____
_____

Recipe:

Rating: ☆☆☆☆☆ **Difficulty:** ☆☆☆☆☆ **Prep Time:**   **Cook Time:**

Ingredients:

Cooking Instructions:

Thoughts and Notes:

Prayer journal

DATE

TODAY'S PASSAGE

PREACHER

SERMON TOPIC

NOTES

PRAYER

KEY VERSES

KEY POINTS

APPLICATION

Notes

Guest List Planner

Name

Address

Telephone Number

E-mail Address

Gift

Save The Day Card Sent	Invitation Sent	R.S.V.P Received	Thank You Sent	Number Attending

Name

Address

Telephone Number

E-mail Address

Gift

Save The Day Card Sent	Invitation Sent	R.S.V.P Received	Thank You Sent	Number Attending

Name

Address

Telephone Number

E-mail Address

Gift

Save The Day Card Sent	Invitation Sent	R.S.V.P Received	Thank You Sent	Number Attending

Name

Address

Telephone Number

E-mail Address

Gift

Save The Day Card Sent	Invitation Sent	R.S.V.P Received	Thank You Sent	Number Attending

Name

Address

Telephone Number

E-mail Address

Gift

Save The Day Card Sent	Invitation Sent	R.S.V.P Received	Thank You Sent	Number Attending

Date:

Quote Of The Day

Today I am truly grateful for...

Here's what would make today great...

I am...

Some amazing things that happened today...

Some amazing things that happened today...

What could I have done to make today even better?

Recipe:

Rating: ☆☆☆☆☆ Difficulty: ☆☆☆☆☆ Prep Time: Cook Time:

Ingredients:

Cooking Instructions:

Thoughts and Notes:

Prayer journal

DATE

TODAY'S PASSAGE   PREACHER   SERMON TOPIC

NOTES

KEY VERSES

PRAYER

KEY POINTS

APPLICATION

Notes

Date:

Quote Of The Day
_____
_____

Today I am truly grateful for...
_____
_____
_____
_____

Here's what would make today great...
_____
_____
_____
_____

I am...
_____
_____
_____

Some amazing things that happened today...
_____
_____

Some amazing things that happened today...
_____
_____

What could I have done to make today even better?
_____
_____

Recipe:

Rating: ☆☆☆☆☆ Difficulty: ☆☆☆☆☆ Prep Time: Cook Time:

Ingredients:

___

Cooking Instructions:

___

Thoughts and Notes:

___

Prayer journal

DATE

TODAY'S PASSAGE   PREACHER   SERMON TOPIC

NOTES

KEY VERSES

PRAYER

KEY POINTS

APPLICATION

Notes

Guest List Planner

Name

Address

Telephone Number

E-mail Address

Gift

Save The Day Card Sent	Invitation Sent	R.S.V.P Received	Thank You Sent	Number Attending

Name

Address

Telephone Number

E-mail Address

Gift

Save The Day Card Sent	Invitation Sent	R.S.V.P Received	Thank You Sent	Number Attending

Name

Address

Telephone Number

E-mail Address

Gift

Save The Day Card Sent	Invitation Sent	R.S.V.P Received	Thank You Sent	Number Attending

Name

Address

Telephone Number

E-mail Address

Gift

Save The Day Card Sent	Invitation Sent	R.S.V.P Received	Thank You Sent	Number Attending

Name

Address

Telephone Number

E-mail Address

Gift

Save The Day Card Sent	Invitation Sent	R.S.V.P Received	Thank You Sent	Number Attending

Date:

Quote Of The Day

Today I am truly grateful for...

Here's what would make today great...

I am...

Some amazing things that happened today...

Some amazing things that happened today...

What could I have done to make today even better?

Recipe:

Rating: ☆☆☆☆☆ Difficulty: ☆☆☆☆☆ Prep Time: Cook Time:

Ingredients:

Cooking Instructions:

Thoughts and Notes:

Prayer journal

DATE

TODAY'S PASSAGE

PREACHER

SERMON TOPIC

NOTES

KEY VERSES

PRAYER

KEY POINTS

APPLICATION

Notes

Date: _____

Quote Of The Day
_____
_____
_____

Today I am truly grateful for...
_____
_____
_____
_____
_____

Here's what would make today great...
_____
_____
_____
_____
_____

I am...
_____
_____
_____

Some amazing things that happened today...
_____
_____

Some amazing things that happened today...
_____
_____

What could I have done to make today even better?
_____
_____

Recipe:

Rating: ☆☆☆☆☆ Difficulty: ☆☆☆☆☆ Prep Time: Cook Time:

Ingredients:

Cooking Instructions:

Thoughts and Notes:

Prayer journal

DATE _____

TODAY'S PASSAGE   PREACHER   SERMON TOPIC

NOTES

_____
_____
_____
_____
_____
_____
_____
_____
_____
_____
_____

KEY VERSES

PRAYER

_____
_____
_____
_____
_____
_____
_____
_____
_____
_____
_____
_____
_____
_____
_____

KEY POINTS

APPLICATION

Notes

Guest List Planner

Name

Address

Telephone Number

E-mail Address

Gift

Save The Day Card Sent	Invitation Sent	R.S.V.P Received	Thank You Sent	Number Attending

Name

Address

Telephone Number

E-mail Address

Gift

Save The Day Card Sent	Invitation Sent	R.S.V.P Received	Thank You Sent	Number Attending

Name

Address

Telephone Number

E-mail Address

Gift

Save The Day Card Sent	Invitation Sent	R.S.V.P Received	Thank You Sent	Number Attending

Name

Address

Telephone Number

E-mail Address

Gift

Save The Day Card Sent	Invitation Sent	R.S.V.P Received	Thank You Sent	Number Attending

Name

Address

Telephone Number

E-mail Address

Gift

Save The Day Card Sent	Invitation Sent	R.S.V.P Received	Thank You Sent	Number Attending

Date:

Quote Of The Day

Today I am truly grateful for...

Here's what would make today great...

I am...

Some amazing things that happened today...

Some amazing things that happened today...

What could I have done to make today even better?

Recipe:

Rating: ☆☆☆☆☆ Difficulty: ☆☆☆☆☆ Prep Time: Cook Time:

Ingredients:
_____
_____
_____
_____
_____
_____

Cooking Instructions:
_____
_____
_____
_____
_____
_____
_____
_____
_____
_____
_____

Thoughts and Notes:
_____
_____
_____
_____
_____

Prayer journal

DATE

TODAY'S PASSAGE   PREACHER   SERMON TOPIC

NOTES

KEY VERSES

PRAYER

KEY POINTS

APPLICATION

Notes

Date:

Quote Of The Day
_____
_____
_____

Today I am truly grateful for...
_____
_____
_____
_____
_____

Here's what would make today great...
_____
_____
_____
_____
_____

I am...
_____
_____
_____

Some amazing things that happened today...
_____
_____

Some amazing things that happened today...
_____
_____

What could I have done to make today even better?
_____
_____

Recipe:

Rating: ☆☆☆☆☆ Difficulty: ☆☆☆☆☆ Prep Time: Cook Time:

Ingredients:

Cooking Instructions:

Thoughts and Notes:

Prayer journal

DATE

TODAY'S PASSAGE   PREACHER   SERMON TOPIC

NOTES

KEY VERSES

PRAYER

KEY POINTS

APPLICATION

Notes

Guest List Planner

Name

Address

Telephone Number

E-mail Address

Gift

| Save The Day Card Sent | Invitation Sent | R.S.V.P Received | Thank You Sent | Number Attending |

Name

Address

Telephone Number

E-mail Address

Gift

| Save The Day Card Sent | Invitation Sent | R.S.V.P Received | Thank You Sent | Number Attending |

Name

Address

Telephone Number

E-mail Address

Gift

| Save The Day Card Sent | Invitation Sent | R.S.V.P Received | Thank You Sent | Number Attending |

Name

Address

Telephone Number

E-mail Address

Gift

| Save The Day Card Sent | Invitation Sent | R.S.V.P Received | Thank You Sent | Number Attending |

Name

Address

Telephone Number

E-mail Address

Gift

| Save The Day Card Sent | Invitation Sent | R.S.V.P Received | Thank You Sent | Number Attending |

Date: _____

Quote Of The Day
_____
_____

Today I am truly grateful for...
_____
_____
_____
_____

Here's what would make today great...
_____
_____
_____
_____

I am...
_____
_____
_____

Some amazing things that happened today...
_____
_____

Some amazing things that happened today...
_____
_____

What could I have done to make today even better?
_____
_____

Recipe:

Rating: ☆☆☆☆☆ Difficulty: ☆☆☆☆☆ Prep Time: Cook Time:

Ingredients:

Cooking Instructions:

Thoughts and Notes:

Prayer journal

DATE

TODAY'S PASSAGE

PREACHER

SERMON TOPIC

NOTES

KEY VERSES

PRAYER

KEY POINTS

APPLICATION

Notes

Date:

Quote Of The Day

Today I am truly grateful for...

Here's what would make today great...

I am...

Some amazing things that happened today...

Some amazing things that happened today...

What could I have done to make today even better?

Recipe:

Rating: ☆☆☆☆☆ Difficulty: ☆☆☆☆☆ Prep Time: Cook Time:

Ingredients:

Cooking Instructions:

Thoughts and Notes:

Prayer journal

DATE

TODAY'S PASSAGE   PREACHER   SERMON TOPIC

NOTES

KEY VERSES

PRAYER

KEY POINTS

APPLICATION

Notes

Guest List Planner

Name
Address
Telephone Number
E-mail Address
Gift

Save The Day Card Sent	Invitation Sent	R.S.V.P Received	Thank You Sent	Number Attending

Name
Address
Telephone Number
E-mail Address
Gift

Save The Day Card Sent	Invitation Sent	R.S.V.P Received	Thank You Sent	Number Attending

Name
Address
Telephone Number
E-mail Address
Gift

Save The Day Card Sent	Invitation Sent	R.S.V.P Received	Thank You Sent	Number Attending

Name
Address
Telephone Number
E-mail Address
Gift

Save The Day Card Sent	Invitation Sent	R.S.V.P Received	Thank You Sent	Number Attending

Name
Address
Telephone Number
E-mail Address
Gift

Save The Day Card Sent	Invitation Sent	R.S.V.P Received	Thank You Sent	Number Attending

Date:

Quote Of The Day

Today I am truly grateful for...

Here's what would make today great...

I am...

Some amazing things that happened today...

Some amazing things that happened today...

What could I have done to make today even better?

Recipe:

Rating: ☆☆☆☆☆ Difficulty: ☆☆☆☆☆ Prep Time: Cook Time:

Ingredients:

Cooking Instructions:

Thoughts and Notes:

Prayer journal

DATE

TODAY'S PASSAGE   PREACHER   SERMON TOPIC

NOTES

KEY VERSES

PRAYER

KEY POINTS

APPLICATION

Notes

Date:

Quote Of The Day

Today I am truly grateful for...

Here's what would make today great...

I am...

Some amazing things that happened today...

Some amazing things that happened today...

What could I have done to make today even better?

Recipe:

Rating: ☆☆☆☆☆ Difficulty: ☆☆☆☆☆ Prep Time: Cook Time:

Ingredients:

Cooking Instructions:

Thoughts and Notes:

Prayer journal

DATE

TODAY'S PASSAGE | PREACHER | SERMON TOPIC

NOTES

PRAYER

KEY VERSES

KEY POINTS

APPLICATION

Notes

Guest List Planner

Name

Address

Telephone Number

E-mail Address

Gift

| Save The Day Card Sent | Invitation Sent | R.S.V.P Received | Thank You Sent | Number Attending |

Name

Address

Telephone Number

E-mail Address

Gift

| Save The Day Card Sent | Invitation Sent | R.S.V.P Received | Thank You Sent | Number Attending |

Name

Address

Telephone Number

E-mail Address

Gift

| Save The Day Card Sent | Invitation Sent | R.S.V.P Received | Thank You Sent | Number Attending |

Name

Address

Telephone Number

E-mail Address

Gift

| Save The Day Card Sent | Invitation Sent | R.S.V.P Received | Thank You Sent | Number Attending |

Name

Address

Telephone Number

E-mail Address

Gift

| Save The Day Card Sent | Invitation Sent | R.S.V.P Received | Thank You Sent | Number Attending |

Date:

Quote Of The Day

___

Today I am truly grateful for...

___

Here's what would make today great...

___

I am...

___

Some amazing things that happened today...

___

Some amazing things that happened today...

___

What could I have done to make today even better?

Recipe:

Rating: ☆☆☆☆☆ Difficulty: ☆☆☆☆☆ Prep Time: Cook Time:

Ingredients:

Cooking Instructions:

Thoughts and Notes:

Prayer journal

DATE

TODAY'S PASSAGE   PREACHER   SERMON TOPIC

NOTES

KEY VERSES

PRAYER

KEY POINTS

APPLICATION

Notes

Date:

Quote Of The Day

Today I am truly grateful for...

Here's what would make today great...

I am...

Some amazing things that happened today...

Some amazing things that happened today...

What could I have done to make today even better?

Recipe:

Rating: ☆☆☆☆☆   Difficulty: ☆☆☆☆☆   Prep Time: Cook Time:

Ingredients:

Cooking Instructions:

Thoughts and Notes:

Prayer journal

DATE

TODAY'S PASSAGE   PREACHER   SERMON TOPIC

NOTES

KEY VERSES

PRAYER

KEY POINTS

APPLICATION

Notes

Guest List Planner

Name

Address

Telephone Number

E-mail Address

Gift

Save The Day Card Sent	Invitation Sent	R.S.V.P Received	Thank You Sent	Number Attending

Name

Address

Telephone Number

E-mail Address

Gift

Save The Day Card Sent	Invitation Sent	R.S.V.P Received	Thank You Sent	Number Attending

Name

Address

Telephone Number

E-mail Address

Gift

Save The Day Card Sent	Invitation Sent	R.S.V.P Received	Thank You Sent	Number Attending

Name

Address

Telephone Number

E-mail Address

Gift

Save The Day Card Sent	Invitation Sent	R.S.V.P Received	Thank You Sent	Number Attending

Name

Address

Telephone Number

E-mail Address

Gift

Save The Day Card Sent	Invitation Sent	R.S.V.P Received	Thank You Sent	Number Attending

Date:

Quote Of The Day

___

Today I am truly grateful for...

___

Here's what would make today great...

___

I am...

___

Some amazing things that happened today...

___

Some amazing things that happened today...

___

What could I have done to make today even better?

Recipe:

Rating: ☆☆☆☆☆ Difficulty: ☆☆☆☆☆ Prep Time: Cook Time:

Ingredients:

Cooking Instructions:

Thoughts and Notes:

Prayer journal

DATE

TODAY'S PASSAGE　　　PREACHER　　　SERMON TOPIC

NOTES

KEY VERSES

KEY POINTS

PRAYER

APPLICATION

Notes

Date: _____

Quote Of The Day
_____
_____
_____

Today I am truly grateful for...
_____
_____
_____
_____
_____
_____

Here's what would make today great...
_____
_____
_____
_____
_____
_____

I am...
_____
_____
_____

Some amazing things that happened today...
_____
_____

Some amazing things that happened today...
_____
_____

What could I have done to make today even better?
_____
_____

Recipe: _____

Rating: ☆☆☆☆☆ Difficulty: ☆☆☆☆☆ Prep Time: _____ Cook Time: _____

Ingredients:

Cooking Instructions:

Thoughts and Notes:

Prayer journal

DATE

TODAY'S PASSAGE   PREACHER   SERMON TOPIC

NOTES

KEY VERSES

KEY POINTS

PRAYER

APPLICATION

Notes

Guest List Planner

Name

Address

Telephone Number

E-mail Address

Gift

Save The Day Card Sent	Invitation Sent	R.S.V.P Received	Thank You Sent	Number Attending

Name

Address

Telephone Number

E-mail Address

Gift

Save The Day Card Sent	Invitation Sent	R.S.V.P Received	Thank You Sent	Number Attending

Name

Address

Telephone Number

E-mail Address

Gift

Save The Day Card Sent	Invitation Sent	R.S.V.P Received	Thank You Sent	Number Attending

Name

Address

Telephone Number

E-mail Address

Gift

Save The Day Card Sent	Invitation Sent	R.S.V.P Received	Thank You Sent	Number Attending

Name

Address

Telephone Number

E-mail Address

Gift

Save The Day Card Sent	Invitation Sent	R.S.V.P Received	Thank You Sent	Number Attending

www.ingramcontent.com/pod-product-compliance
Lightning Source LLC
Chambersburg PA
CBHW070723170125
20526CB00030B/867